Managing Money Made Easy

Ultimate guide that will change the way you manage your money

AMARPREET SINGH

Publisher - The Thought Flame

info@thethoughtflame.com

www.thethoughtflame.com

Table of Contents

Introduction

Since the beginning of the Great Recession, gallons of ink have been spilled trying to create cosmic justice for past sins and present economic inequities. For those of us damaged by the disaster, much of that passion feels like wasted time and energy. This isn't one of those books. This book is for the disheartened reader who, for whatever reason, is having trouble remembering their life before they felt financially out of control. While this book offers no solutions to make corporations behave like decent, ethical "people," it does offer a simple, clear path toward a more stable financial existence for those willing to accept it.

Readers of all income levels can find its simple financial plan useful. However, since this book focuses on doing your very best with your current income, readers looking for discussions on long term planning or investments might be disappointed. Don't misunderstand: long term planning is vital for financial stability, but there are so many other great books on the topic we won't deal with those topics here. So if your concerns revolve around what will happen to your child's financial aid when you gift them a large portfolio of stocks, this book may have little to offer you. On the other hand, if your concerns revolve around how to make sure you can afford to pay the mortgage on an upside down house so your child has a roof over his or her head, this book is written for you.

If you have read other personal finance books, I hope you aren't disappointed to find this one a little bit different. Many, but not all, personal finance books offer what I call the bowl of popcorn approach to financial advice. They are full of little chewy nuggets of information which may or may not be useful on a daily basis. Very few of them offer a single coherent financial plan stretched throughout the book. There are notable exceptions; my aim is to be among them.

If you are going to benefit from this book, you and I will have to agree that lasting change takes more than simply changing what you do . Lasting change also requires that you alter what you believe about money. To me, changing what you do without changing what you believe is very similar to dieting. The weight comes off, but unless you come to believe that healthy foods can satisfy your cravings better than junk food the diet won't work. As soon as your diet ends, you will go right back to eating the way you ate before and end up putting the weight back on.

The same holds true with financial changes. I can teach you how to avoid impulse purchases at the grocery story, but that won't help you if your belief system about money is broken. You will just impulse buy online instead.

The plan I offer isn't pie-in-the-sky idealism either. This is the battle-hardened financial plan which has guided my family for years. It is also the same plan I preached to other families as a real estate agent, financial advisor and financial counselor. It is deeply personal for me, and I know it can change the way you deal with money and relieve your stress.

So, what are you waiting for? Let's get started.

Chapter One: How To Ease The Money Problem

It's normal to spend money on a daily basis, but what's not normal is not noticing that some of these expenses are actually more impulsive than necessary. In this book, you will learn about the simplest ways to save money, what are the usual culprits for not being able to save, and further tips on cutting costs efficiently.

Nobody really likes to waste money. If given a clean chance to, you would really like to save or set aside money for more important things. What people have trouble with is finding that "clean chance" to start saving. Oftentimes there are small windows opening, giving way to a chance to save up . However, 90% of the time people fail to take it. Why do people fail to take the small and frequent chances to save up?

Why Saving Money Is Important?

1. Saving For Your Future

It's common for people to put off saving because they are either already in the middle of a financial crisis or simply caught up in a shopping spree. It could also be said that people don't feel financially secure, so they think that starting to save might just make things difficult.

What happens is the development of this mindset – "I can start later." Sometimes, this "later" never comes , or when it does, there are emergencies and other more pressing financial matters need attention. In the end, there's really no better time to start saving than now.

By saving money as soon as possible you will never have to worry about not having money set aside for emergencies in the future. The money that you can save will not only help you in the case of an emergency, but you can begin storing that money for you retirement fund and have that money readily available right when you need it.

2. Become Financially Independent

People with families are not the only ones who should think about saving money. At some point in your life, you will grow old, become obsolete in your career or simply experience financial difficulties. During these trying times, you will wish you had some "backup" stored up somewhere to help you survive. Aside from that, just because you are flying solo, it doesn't mean that the things you buy impulsively doesn't add up to much.

It might surprise you but most single (not in a relationship) individuals spend twice as much, if not equivalent, as a person who has children or a family. Weekly take-out dinners, designer clothes, exclusive DVD sets, and entertainment systems are infinitely more expensive than a month's worth of diapers.

Saving money will allow you to buy all of the things that you want, while still ensuring that you aren't struggling to pay your monthly bills. Who doesn't want the chance to have all of their bills paid, but still have two to three grand still left over.

3. The Ability To Live Comfortably

Most people think of small bills as insignificant because, well, they are small or have less value and would not really be of any use in emergencies . The truth is, they are actually the most significant portion of the idea of "savings".

Small amounts are what a person builds up and turns into millions. Mountains are not made of singular gigantic boulders. They are made of sand, stones, rocks and some boulders. In the financial comparison of mountains to savings, it's the pennies that make up the base and not the hundreds.

When you save money wisely you will never have to worry about suffering through paycheck to paycheck. You can rest assured that if there is ever a situation where you need money quick, you can simply dip into your savings to cover your expenses without stressing about it beforehand.

How To Allocate Your Income Wisely

1. Creating Your Household Monthly Expenses

While you are tracking your expenses, you will need to gather all the information together to get your budget started. First, determine your income.

How much does each adult bring home after taxes? Does a teenager contribute to the family finances in any way? Do you have someone living with you and paying rent? Does anyone receive SSI, disability, or payments of another kind? Add up all the income for each person contributing and then you'll know what you have coming in each month.

Make a list of everything you spend money on each month. This would include housing (rent or mortgage), insurance (homeowner's, rental, car, life), utilities (electric, water, gas, cell and home phone), creditors (major credit card companies as well as department or specialty stores), and groceries. Don't forget about the Internet, entertainment (satellite or cable television), property taxes, automobile upkeep (gasoline and maintenance), charitable giving, savings, and family gifts throughout the year.

2. Know Your Due Dates

First of all, do you pay your bills on time each month? This is often the first sign of a spending problem. Rather than using the money earned at their job to take care of their living obligations, people with spending problems choose to spend money on things they want. They may feel they "deserve" the consumer items they purchase as a reward for their work, and don't budget at all for these items. They buy on the spur of the moment instead of waiting to purchase it until they have the money saved.

If you are paying late every month, you need to look at your organization or pattern of spending. And don't forget, one late payment to the credit card companies can do untold damage to your credit score. Therefore, stay on top of the bills, no matter how stressful the statements can be at the end of each month.

3. Deposit Some Of Your Check Into Your Bank Account

You may want to consider having your pay direct deposited. This option, offered by many companies around the country, allows you to receive your pay without having to wait for a physical check . It is also deposited into your chosen account so you have access to it without having to run to the bank, wait in line, or possibly miss depositing your check entirely.

This also gives you the option to leave some of that money in your bank account. As a rule I highly recommend to leaving at least 10% of your check in your account at all times. While this may not seem like much at first, the amount will slowly add up over time.

4. Pay Yourself First

Of course there are many of us who want to spend our money on the things that we like and want such as a new TV, a fancy dinner, a brand new phone or even a vacation. Of course not all of us can afford those things but that does not mean that you don't deserve to leave yourself some money so that you can spend on little things that you enjoy.

That is why I recommend that every time you get paid set aside between $20-$50 just for yourself. Spend that money on whatever pleases you whether it is to see a favorite movie or to order take out. Do whatever you want with it. You deserve it.

How To Practice Smart Spending Habits

When economic times are good, people rarely consider how their current spending habits can affect their future financial outlook if things ever take a turn for the worse. People may think they have more than enough to live on, until the unthinkable happens.

By following smart spending strategies, families may be able to not only survive an economic down turn; they may also be able to thrive and create their own emergency fund that will be able to help them get through any more really rough times in one piece.

In this section you will leave the basics of smart spending and learn for yourself how to spend the right way.

1. Do Not Bring Your Credit Cards With You All Of The Time

Do you use credit cards to pay for everything? Once the habit has begun of using credit cards to pay for everything, problems generally begin. This may mean you are using credit cards for everything from groceries to your utilities. But because you are putting everything on credit you may not be aware of exactly how much you're spending each month.

In other cases, you may really be overspending and living beyond your means. In this case, you will know it. It can often result in things like shopping and then stuffing the bags into the closet without ever even looking at the items.

Sit down and look at all of your most recent statements and see what you are spending money on. Itemize them into categories, similar to tax categories. Where is most of your money going? If it is to food and you have a large family, think about clipping coupons or ways to cut corners. If it is on consumer luxury items, you need to start spending smart.

If you are using the cards without even thinking about them, locate your lowest interest card through looking at your statements, and put that back in your wallet. As for your other credit cards, simply toss them out or put them in a location where you will not be able to use them for anything. The less credit cards you have with you, the less likely you are to use them to spend on every day things and the more money you will save yourself in the long run.

2. Spend Your Money On Things That You Need Rather Than The Things That You Want

It's really difficult to listen to friends, family, or co-workers talk about all the new things they have just bought themselves . Maybe they bought a new car, a large screen television, or something else you've really been yearning for. Even though you'd like to own the same things, there's nothing that says you have to. You don't have to fall into the mindset that you must "keep up with the Forman's."

The best thing that you can do is to look for other ways you can reduce spending by going through your budget. Obviously some things on your budget are fixed expenses, but even with those, if you check carefully, you may be able to find ways to save.

When shopping always ask yourself the question, "Do I really need this? Is it really that important that I can waste this money on it?" If the question is no, simply do not buy the item and walk away as fast as possible from it to reduce the temptation.

3. Do Not Give In To Your Kids Request

You know children today. They seem to want nearly everything that they see on TV or whatever their friends have. If your children always ask for you to buy them their favorite toy, a new gaming console or a new video game, if you simply do not have the money do not give in to their requests.

However, there are exceptions to this rule. If your child needs money for school lunch or to participate in a school event, then of course you should give them the money they need. Always go with your gut on this and just ask yourself the same question suggested above and stick with it.

Ways To Identify Between The Wants and Needs

Your essentials are rent/ mortgage, utilities, and food, with transportation another essential for most people, but with various options.

The key thing to note here is that with the exception of the mortgage or rent, all of these expenses are flexible. In other words, it is up to you to control your spending. You CAN save on electricity, gas and cell phone bills if you know how.

You can choose between owning a fancy car, one that will get you from A to B, or public transportation or car pooling. You will find that almost everything is negotiable these days, and you can get incredible bargains on essentials online too if you look carefully enough.

Food is a growing expense due to rising prices, but cutting coupons can help you save big . So can going to every store in the area to shop only for the loss leaders. Just make sure you only buy the sale item if you actually use or need it.

Try to get the best prices on everything, from back to school supplies, to planning your wedding. Rather than making a purchase as soon as you see something you want, create a list of items you'd like to purchase, something along the lines of the Wish List on Amazon . Then set up a separate bank account you can pay yourself into. If possible, make it a savings account with a debit card linked to it, which can be used as a credit card such as MasterCard, but only if you have enough money in the account.

Chapter Two: How To Save For Your Future

Do you ever wonder why some people seem so well -off that their biggest problem is figuring out how they will spend their money? No matter how much they spend, it seems like their money just keeps growing. Are you looking forward to finally retiring from your job and doing the things that you have always wanted to do but have no time for? Have you always wanted to invest but you are not particularly sure how to go about it?

What Is Investing?

Investment experts define investing as "the act of committing money or capital to an endeavor with the expectation of obtaining an additional income or profit." To put it in simpler terms, investing basically means using money as leverage by letting it work for you. The keyword here is leverage. Instead of you working hard from morning to night to earn money, you invest your money so it can earn more money even when you are not doing any work at all. Investing is actually an old concept but not many people have taken full advantage of it.

You may know someone from the older generation who preaches that the only way you can earn money is by getting yourself employed. Up until now, the majority of our population is still doing that exact thing— working for money. But there's one big flaw in this mindset: if you want to increase your income to upgrade your lifestyle, your only option is to work longer hours. We all know that we only have a limited number of hours to work every day. Moreover , you need to strike a balance between work and your other priorities such as your family and health.

Since there is a limit to the number of hours you can effectively work in a day, you need to use leverage —something you can do to expand your earning capacity without requiring more working hours from you. You may want to earn more money even if you are working for your employer or even when you are sleeping or spending time with your family. You can do this by letting money do the work for you through investing. You can expect to receive additional income even if you don't work overtime or get a raise from your boss.

There are actually several options for you to make an investment. You can invest your money in stocks, government bonds, mutual funds, and even real estate. Even starting a small business can be considered a form of investment. These different ways to invest are commonly called "investment vehicles." Each of these investment vehicles has its own pros and cons which will be discussed in a later chapter. However, no matter what investment vehicle you choose, your goal will always be the same and that is to earn extra income. This may sound obvious but it is one significant concept that you should fully comprehend.

Things That Are Worth Investing In

Now that you understand what investing is, the next thing to do is to pick the type of investments that suit your financial goals and risk profile. Below are some of the most popular type of investments that novice investor can begin with.

1. Forex

For a novice investor it is advised to stay away from dynamic and volatile investment called currency exchange or better known as Forex. This investment is highly volatile because it is tagged in the currency market. Currencies usually fluctuate every minute. The reward in forex trading can be very substantial, far better than what the traditional investments could offer (stocks, bonds). You can double or even triple your investment within a week, a day or even hours.

However, if you are trading against the market, your investment could lose significantly on a very short notice. There is a very good chance that your investment could be wiped out if you invest in the currency market without fully understanding it. Hence, it is advised that you invest in the forex market with proper guidance and knowledge. Also, only invest the capital that you are willing to risk. For a beginner like you , it is advisable to stick with the more common and relatively stable types of investment like stocks, bonds and mutual funds.

2. Bonds

Bond is a fixed income type of investment. It usually carries a low risk compared to stocks and other alternative investments. Bonds are secured and stable. It is a debt securities issued by the government, a start-up company or a blue chip. By purchasing bonds you become one of the creditors of the organization that issues them. A bond holder is paid a fixed or floating interest at a certain period of time. The principal will also be paid in full at a predetermined schedule.

Bonds carry a very low risk. However, since the issuers of these securities are stable organizations, they only pay a very low return. Moderate and conservative type of investors usually invests in the bond market.

3. Insurance

Insurance is different from other types of investment. Its goal, compared to others, is not wealth creation but, rather, asset protection. Insurance protects you, your assets, and other investments from fortuitous events like accidents, acts of God, and other unforeseen events.

If you invest in a real property, fire and earth quake insurance will protect your homes in the event that those calamities and disasters consume your asset. You will be paid accordingly once your real property is properly insured. You can also use insurance with your other possessions like cars, motorcycles, among others.

Health and life insurance are personal insurance that protect the most important of all investments- yourself and your family. Health insurance covers your hospital bills and medicines in the event you suffer a grave illness. A life insurance protects the well-being of your family in case something bad happen to you. A certain amount will then be paid to your loved ones.

4. Mutual Funds

It is a pool of funds being managed by professional fund managers. These fund managers have different strategies. Some are focused in secured and stable companies, others are focused on start-ups and technology related companies, and some funds concentrate on bonds and government securities. Other funds focused on both the stock and bonds market.

Mutual funds are perfect for moderate to conservative type of investors. It is also popular to novice investors. The logic is that they could get better returns by having a professional to manage their investments.

5. Stocks

Investing in stocks is one of the most, if not the most , popular type of investments. The success and even failure of the stock market over time give rise to its unprecedented popularity. When you purchase and invest in stocks you become part owner of the company that issues it. Hence , you have the right to receive a share in the company's profit in the form of dividends.

Stocks can be a very rewarding investment. In fact, many stock investors become rich. However, an equal amount of investors become broker investing in the stock market. While you are entitled to be paid dividends , not all companies pay it regularly . Most of them could not pay dividends to their investors for a prolonged period of time. Moreover, the value of your stock investment could drop dramatically making a huge loss on your investment.

Stocks are ideal for investors with huge risk capital. Investors who are risk takers are the common participants of the stock market.

Why Is It Important To Set Up A Retirement Fund?

Did you know that one-third of adult Filipinos recently said that they were not preparing for retirement? After a recent survey conducted by a financial research group, it was found that about 36% of adults have said they have not yet started saving for retirement. Even worse, more than a quarter of those questioned were near the age of 50 to 64.

What are some of the reasons why people don't plan for retirement?

The main reason is procrastination . When you are living paycheck to paycheck, it is very difficult for you to consider putting aside money. Usually they say they will wait until they get a raise before they start saving. Another reason is simply because most adults do not make enough money to cover all of their bills. You know how hard the economy is today. It is harder now more than ever to make ends meet at the end of the month and even harder to make the money that you need to begin saving in the first place.

What if you lose your job? What kind of job could you expect to get when you are past sixty or seventy? As painful as it may be, it is important to face these considerations now, while you are still earning money and able to save a nest egg that you can draw upon when and if you have decided to retire. Obviously, the early you start the better, but even at an advanced age you can still put aside enough to maintain a decent standard of living in your retirement. Even making small lifestyle changes that enable you to put some money away for the future can greatly help.

In this section you will learn different ways that will help you start with your retirement planning by taking you through everything you need to consider, from figuring out how much you will need to maintain your desired standard of living to the best way to create a retirement portfolio that will continue to generate an income even after you have retired.

Why Save For An Emergency Fund

It simply does not matter how much money you make every year or how well you plan things out in your life, eventually something bad will happen. That is just the nature of things.

Think of it this way: what happens if your hot water heater springs a leak and floods your basement? Or what happens if your car breaks down on the side of the highway? Or what happens if a beloved family member comes down with a serious illness.

Regardless of what happens, all of these scenarios requires you to have money readily available. So, how can an emergency fund help you in the case of an emergency?

An emergency fund is essentially money that you stash away for the sole purpose of having access to it later when you have an emergency. This kind of fund should be easily accessible like a hiding place in your house or a savings account with your local bank. Regardless of where you decide to put it, it should be stored somewhere where you can grab it without any kind of penalty or fee and that you can access within a day or two.

Without an emergency fund you will not only create more financial stress on yourself, but it can also drive you into serious debt if you are not careful enough. In our unpredictable economy it is important to have an emergency fund set up so you have all of your bases covered before anything bad can happen to you.

Why Should You Add Insurance To Your Emergency Fund?

Insurance is like a backup plan that an individual or group can fall back on in cases of unexpected financial losses such as accidents, illness, and theft, to name a few.

In order to manage risks, the insurance policy transfers any possible loss an insured person may experience to the insurance company. In return, the insured person pays a premium. Because of insurance, businesses , organizations , and individuals are protected against such losses and monetary difficulties by paying premiums periodically.

People who don't want to experience financial difficulties can take advantage of insurance benefits. A person may acquire insurance to protect his family when the insured dies. He can also ensure that any debts or contingent liabilities will be repaid even after death. An employer may buy insurance for his key employees to protect his business in case one of his trusted employees dies. He might insure himself so that he has money to buy out his partners at the time of his death so the whole equity can be owned by his family. He can also insure his business so that it is protected from any income loss due to business interruption.

A person can protect himself from any unexpected health expenses. He can protect his home against flood, fire, theft, and other unforeseen hazards. He can even protect himself against lawsuits. In case of disability, insurance can provide monetary benefits to the family of the insured. A vehicle can be insured against losses or theft due to accidents.

Health Insurance

Health insurance is important because any accident or illness can wipe out any financial savings a person may have. At times, he may even be in debt because of the high cost of treatment. A health insurance policy can take care of medical expenses. In return, the insured must pay premiums periodically.

Like the other kinds of insurance, health insurance has its limitations and exclusions. The insurance policy usually includes such components. If the medical procedure isn't included in the insurance coverage, the insured must pay for it out of pocket. Health insurance can be purchased from an insurance agent or broker. However, most individuals obtain health insurance through their employers.

A health insurance policy involves some costs. Premiums are paid by the insured to ensure that his policy is in force and that he can claim it when needed. A deductible is money which the insured pays out of his pocket. In general, if the insured wants to pay lower premiums, he must pay a higher deductible. Co-insurance is expenses paid by the insurance company. It is usually in the form of a percentage. A co-payment, on the other hand, is the maximum amount the insured has to pay for every medical expense . It is not part of the deductible. The stop-loss limit is the maximum co-insurance limit . When this limit is reached, the insurer has to pay for all medical expenses incurred by the insured.

Health insurance can have different forms. It can be an indemnity plan, health maintenance organization, preferred provider organization, or point of service. An indemnity plan reimburses the individual for medical expenses based on a schedule. It includes medical coverage, surgical expenses, and hospital confinement. The insurer pays the insured a fixed amount on a daily basis as long as the number of days doesn't exceed the maximum preset number of days.

Life Insurance

Life insurance was introduced to protect the income of households during the phase of wealth accumulation. Currently, it is being used for estate tax planning and wealth preservation. It provides for the surviving members of the family so that they can go on with their lives even after the death of the insured. It is now considered a planning tool. However, individuals shouldn't regard it as a savings scheme, because there are better savings vehicles in which they can invest their money.

Life insurance premiums are paid either annually, quarterly, or monthly during the duration of the insurance term. An insured person who died during the term of the insurance can be assured that his family will receive the whole insurance amount. Ancient Rome is believed to have kept the first life insurance records. It was Edmond Halley, the astronomer, who devised the early actuarial tables in the late 17th century. The tables were used to compute the insurance risk of a person based on mortality rate. In essence, a person pays higher premiums when the insurer faces higher risks in ensuring them.

In order to calculate risks, an individual needs to answer a questionnaire about his medical history, his travel habits, his driving record, and his credit history, as well as his hobbies and lifestyle. Insurance actuaries then compute the premiums he needs to pay. In general, life insurance premiums are based on the present medical conditions, sex, and age of the insured. Older individuals pay more premiums. Men also pay greater premiums than women. Those individuals who have a family history of cancer or heart disease, mental illness, high blood pressure, and heart conditions also pay greater premiums. People who engage in dangerous activities like scuba diving or skydiving pay a higher insurance rate. Smokers are also charged higher premiums.

In order to claim against a life insurance policy, the beneficiary must file a claim with the insurer. He will have to provide the insured's death certificate, as well as the original insurance policy. After processing the claim, the insurance company pays a lump sum to the beneficiary. There are cases when a claim is denied, especially when fraud is involved.

There are different types of life insurance: whole life, universal life, variable life, variable universal life, and term life. A whole life policy guarantees insurance for the duration of the insured's life. Often, the insurance policy accumulates cash value, which is guaranteed up to the time the policy is surrendered. Death benefits are guaranteed, and premiums remain constant during the insurance term. In whole life policies, a part of the insurance premium is applied to the insurance, administrative expenses, and the investment. The interest generated by the investment part is often tax-free, unless it is withdrawn. The withdrawal may be tax-free if it hasn't exceeded the total amount of premiums paid minus any previous withdrawals or dividends paid. A whole life insurance policy charges higher premiums than other kinds of life insurance because of its cash build-up feature. The cash earned by the insurance can be used to pay the remaining premiums.

Chapter Three: Signs That You Are Drained Financially

No one wants to admit they have problems with making ends meet, much less admitting to having excessive spending habits. They would like to believe that their spending is normal and under control. That they might splurge a little now and again, but they are in control.

In some cases they might be right. In other cases, they may have a serious spending problem that they will need to come to grips with. So how do you know if you actually have a spending problem?

Why Are You Unable To Make Ends Meet?

There can be a variety of factors that can lead you to have trouble making ends meet. Some of us simply have too many bills to pay, working jobs that do not pay the desired hourly rate, busy paying off student loans, car payments, etc.

If you are struggling just to make ends meet and you are living paycheck to paycheck, you know how tough it is. There are many factors that can point to you struggling financially such as:

1. Literally living paycheck to paycheck and going through what you have earned in two weeks in less than a day.

2. Most or all of your money is directed only to paying bills.

3. You have no money at the end of the month to spend on whatever it is that you want.

4. You have more bills than you can even pay.

5. You are beginning to use your credit cards to pay your bills.

6. You recently lost your job.

7. You do not make enough money to cover all of your bills.

How To Tell If You Spend Money "Emotionally"

Have you ever found yourself spending money without any rhyme or reason behind it? Have you found that you often have no money at the end of every payday? In this section you will learn exactly how you spend emotionally and if you are doing it to feed a deeper need.

Have you ever:

1. Bought something simply because one of your friends had it?

2. Have you ever bought something simply because you have the money to do it?

3. Have you ever neglected your budget to buy something that you have always wanted?

4. Have you ever blown your entire paycheck just by shopping and purchasing random items?

If you have answered yes to any of these questions, the chances are that you are spending emotionally. The reason behind these random moments of spending could be anything from curing your depression to filling your need of jealousy or envy. Either way spending your money in an emotional fashion can lead to difficult financial problems in the future.

Are You In Danger of Losing Your Home?

Instead of having collection companies calling your home to pay your credit cards, do you find that you are receiving phone calls from your mortgage lenders? Do you find yourself behind on rent? In these cases, most people will refuse for you to end up homeless, but if you are spending more money than you actually have, the sole responsibility of the situation that you find yourself in will rest squarely on your own shoulders.

So far we have discussed a variety of reasons as to why it may be tough to make ends meet and to pay all of your bills on time, such as losing your job or simply not making enough money. However, for some people it may be due to the fact that they simply have bad spending habits. If this is the case you need to take a step back and look at the kind of relationship that you have with money already and get yourself back on track financially.

Remember, your home is perhaps the most important financial investment that you will make in your life. If you find that you have mortgage lenders on your back, it is important that you are not tempted by random consolidation offers where most lenders will ask you to use your home as a security deposit. While this may solve your credit issues in some cases, it can also cause a variety of other problems such as homelessness or foreclosures, especially if you cannot meet the bill due date.

Have You Ever Considered Trying To File For Bankruptcy?

There are many people out there that believe filing for bankruptcy is the way to fix all of their problems, especially if they are drowning in debt. While it may give you the chance at a fresh start and to get rid of all of your financial issues, it will cause more problems than you will be able to handle. This may have been the case many years ago, but now it is much harder to write off your bad debts than you may realize.

Today there is no such thing as an easy bankruptcy. Not only will you need a good lawyer to handle your case, but you will then have to go into a payment plan just to pay off your lawyer in the end.

Of course there are many creditors out there who will try to make a deal with you for a lesser amount, in the end you will have to pay off every single one of your debts in as structured a way as possible. For example, if you owe back taxes, you will need to have your wages garnish until you pay off what you owe. While this may seem ok, in the end you will have to deal with whatever money you have left over and try to make ends meet as best as you can.

One of the biggest consequences of bankruptcy today is that it will mess up your credit history in the long run. On top of that it will also affect what kind of jobs you can apply for in the future such as government jobs. Think of bankruptcy as what labels bad credit today. It will be much harder for you to find a job, finance a car, finance a house and applying for credit cards in the future.

Remember, bankruptcy may seem like the best solution for now, especially if you want to get the creditors and mortgage lenders to stop calling your home, but in the end it will just cause an array of problems for you. Before even thinking about bankruptcy you need to take a step back and look at your entire financial situation as a whole and come up with ways to get yourself out of that rut before filing for bankruptcy.

Chapter Four: How To Manage Your Credit Cards

Some people who spend excessively don't have a problem with actual cash in their hands. They do, however, have a tendency to spend without thought when it comes to using credit cards. It may not matter to them if they have a large balance and are paying interest for it each month. So long as they get to spend, they don't really think much about their spending until their credit card is declined in a shop, or they get a past due call or notice.

Knowing what triggers you to overspend is a great step to getting your spending under control. Learn self-control when it comes to using your credit cards , or cash in hand , and you can begin to see light at the end of the financial tunnel.

Why You Should Use Credit Cards If You Cannot Pay Them Off In The Future

Is there such a thing as credit card addiction? Can someone really be addicted to using these plastics that have exorbitant interest rates? The answer to both of these questions is "Yes". Credit card addiction and compulsive shopping are interrelated, because many compulsive shoppers use their credit cards to pay for their purchases.

Credit card addiction is the overwhelming desire to buy things that you may or may not need using your credit card. This can potentially ruin your finances in the end, because when your debt starts to build up, your income will no longer be enough to pay for it and you will end up bankrupt. Compulsive shoppers use credit cards to feed their shopping obsession. This is because it is more difficult to spend hard-earned cash that you have in your wallet than to spend borrowed money contained in a plastic card.

To be able to treat your credit card addiction and eliminate debt, you first need to know if you really have the condition. You need to observe your credit card usage to identify potential red flags that could mean shopping addiction using your credit card. If you can observe any of these warning signs, you may be suffering from credit card addiction:

1. Buying These That You Do Not Need

This is one that you really need to look out for and that is one red flag that you need to look out for. Because of this, you end up with a lot of stuff at home that you do not really use and only end up collecting dust at the back of your closet or under your bed. You are also tempted to buy unnecessary items just because they are on sale.

2. Hiding Your Purchases From Those You Love

When you hide your purchases from your spouse, parents, or other close family members, it could also be a sign that you have credit card addiction because you know that what you are doing is not something to be proud of. You know that you are doing something wrong, which gives you that guilty feeling and is the reason why you hide your purchases.

3. Having Maxed Out Credit Cards

Another warning sign is when most or all of your credit cards are maxed out, which means that you have reached your credit cards' limit and you can no longer use them to make purchases unless you pay at least the minimum.

How To Reduce The Temptation To Use Your Credit Cards

You first need to know some short-term solutions that can help you treat your credit card addiction. These will help you overcome those urges to shop using your credit card. You can turn some of these into habits that can ultimately help you eliminate debt. It is important to stick to these tips and strategies if you want to get positive results.

The first few days or even weeks can really be difficult and will really test your willpower and discipline. However, if you really want to overcome your credit card addiction and get rid of debt, then you need to be consistent in doing the solutions presented in this chapter. Here are some short-term strategies that can help you get rid of debt and stop credit card addiction.

1. Cut Up Your Credit Cards

Some people simply put their credit cards inside the freezer and leave them inside a block of ice while other simply put their credit card at the bottom of their sock drawer. For people who have credit card addiction, these strategies may not work because they still have ways to access the credit card.

They can simply use a hammer to break the ice and get their credit card or they can just rummage through their sock drawer whenever they have the urge to shop. This is why the best tip is to just cut your credit card in half because no store in this world will accept a cut up credit card. One important thing to remember though is to avoid closing your account because this can do damage to your credit report.

2. Don't Be Afraid To Leave Your Wallet Behind

If you love the experience of browsing through different shops and looking at their colorful displays, but you always end up buying things that you do not really need, then you should consider leaving your wallet behind and go window shopping instead. This way, you have no way to pay for items, thereby preventing you from buying anything. You can browse through different shops all you want without feeling stressed out and anxious, because there is no need to control yourself and your urge to buy since you do not have your wallet with you.

3. Avoid Being Tempted

Although it is a great idea to just leave your wallet at home if you want to visit your favorite shops , it is even better to just simply avoid being near these temptations that may trigger your desire to go shopping and use your credit card. If you can help it, do not go to shopping malls, discount warehouses and other places that will attract you to buy. You should not visit shopping websites and you should also throw away any shopping catalogues where you might find something that you absolutely must buy.

When you travel to other places, do not splurge too much on shopping for souvenirs or exotic items that you do not really like. If you want to have a lot of souvenirs, then you should take a lot of pictures instead; these are absolutely free!

Chapter Five: How To Stay Out of Debt Now and Forever

If you are in debt, do not worry. You can easily overcome it. If you do not overcome debt there are many things that you will lose such as precious time and valuable money. Remember, if you only pay the minimum payment every month for your credit cards, it will take you many years to pay off all of your debt due to the ridiculous interest rates. It has been proven that more money is spent on interest rates than the actual monetary amount of the debt that you owe.

So why pay off your debt if you are going to lose money in the process anyway? Because you need to look at your debt as a financial obligation. Also you will want to pay off your debts to avoid suffering from more financial troubles in the future such as a bad credit rating and a negative credit history.

How To Tell If You Are Living Above Your Means

Debt elimination is a lengthy process. It's the opposite of how fast and easy it was to incur them. It involves a lot of paperwork . You will need lawyers and financial advisors in some cases; such services entail additional expenses on your part. The process could be more difficult and lengthier if you have no plans at all.

Basically, what you need to do is follow the steps below. These will help you manage your debts better.

1. Determine your personality when it comes to financial matters.

2. Evaluate the severity of your debts.

3. Assess your finances.

4. Devise a plan, specifically a repayment scheme.

5. Carry out your plan.

The first step deals with how you spend your money before. You need to realize the mistakes you did that led to your debt issues. Ask yourself questions and be honest with yourself. Did your car serve you well? Do you really need all of those appliances and furniture? Do you save? Recognize and admit that you made bad decisions when it comes to purchasing and saving.

Cutting Down On Your Unnecessary Expenses

You will also need to determine between your needs and wants, especially if you are living above your needs. What you perceive as your needs may simply be wants for other people and vice versa. That's why it is unwise for you to comment on the manner at which other people prioritize their expenses. In this case, it is always best for you to focus on your own finances and find the answer to whether a certain expense of yours is classified as a want or a need.

A need is essentially defined as something that you cannot live without. Food, water, and electricity are only of a few examples of what needs in today's world are. Because these are needs, you can't simply afford to miss them in your budget.

On the other hand, wants are those that you can live without. A second car, a new smartphone, or gaming consoles are only a few examples. Because these are wants, you can certainly let them go and go back to get them when you already have surplus money.

So why is it important to distinguish between your needs and your wants? The answer lies in determining your financial priorities. At this point, you can't afford to indulge on your wants when you know that your debts are out there waiting to be paid. Soon, you'll be able to spend the money exactly the way you want it, too – that's after you get rid of your debts.

Are You Financially Stable Enough Before You Start Helping Out Others?

We all know how hard the times are today. There is hardly a person out there that can lie about struggling to pay their own bills or struggling to go out and enjoy themselves once in a while. For those of us who are generous, we can't help but want to help those we care about get out of their financial issues. However, if you are struggling to make ends meet yourself, you need to ask yourself if you are financially stable enough to lend out money.

Some of the questions that can point to you being unstable financially are:

1. If I lend out money, will I be able to pay all of my bills at the beginning of the month?

2. If I lend out money, can the person pay me back before I will actually need it?

3. Is the person I am lending out money too trustworthy and will they pay me back?

4. Do I really have the money needed to lend out?

If you have answered no to any of those questions, the simple thing to do in this circumstance is to keep your money and avoid lending it out. Remember, you and your bills must come first. While it may seem mean and cruel, you are the one who must come first and your bills are your first priority.

Chapter Six: Ways To Save A Single Cent

Saving money daily can actually come as easily as eating breakfast or deciding to walk instead of taking the bus to school. What's difficult is realizing these small ways of saving money. It's easy to overlook something so simple, and mistake it for something tacky or menial. In saving money, these simple and daily acts won't just keep your bill neatly in your wallet, they might also double it by the end of the week.

Here are the simplest and most overlooked ways to save money today that once you begin using them, you will be surprised to find out how much money you can come up with at the end of the month.

1. When In Doubt, Fold It and Put It In Your Pocket

One of the best and most commonly quoted advice about saving money is this: Take your money and fold it into your pocket. In reality, literally, folding your money bill in half won't double its amount. However, the total value of what you have can and will be doubled for each day you follow this habit successfully. If, for example, in each day you set aside five something and by the end of the week you should be able to ad $35 to your savings.

Folding your money over or simply keeping it in your pocket won't just save you some money, it will help control those shopping impulses. One of the most common mistakes people make when they get their money on payday is splurging. It's no surprise if you can relate to a scene like this – pay day arrives and you feel as rich as a king. It only takes a week, or less, of seemingly endless wealth until you're broke or nearly broke.

By the end of the month, you're sulking, cutting down expenses and waiting at the edge of your seat for the next payday. The cycle happens and it will continue to happen over and over again until you decide to act upon it.

2. Save Every Penny That You Have

Most people think of small bills as insignificant because, well, they are small or have less value and would not really be of any use in emergencies . The truth is, they are actually the most significant portion of the idea of "savings."

Small amounts are what a person builds up and turns into millions. Mountains are not made of singular gigantic boulders. They are made of sand, stones, rocks and some boulders. In the financial comparison of mountains to savings, it's the pennies that make up the base and not the hundreds. While saving pennies wont make you rich, it will change your relationship with money. If you practice putting your coins in a tin every day, you will condition yourself to save. This brings us to the next overlooked technique in saving money, for long- or short-term purposes.

3. Start Out Small and Start Right Now

Starting small is the easiest way to save, but starting small is belittled by most because of the expected value it achieves. "Every little bit counts," that's one saying that applies to a lot of things, including saving money. Since the idea of saving up is a continuous and consistent habit, even the small contributions add up to the pile. It's also easy to save by starting small, because it gives people enough freedom to buy the things they need or want. It won't feel like such a responsibility, which will lengthen its chances of actually growing to be a successful habit.

The benefit is simple, relating to saving each penny. The sooner you start saving, no matter how small the beginnings, the more chances you'd have to accumulate your wealth.

4. Develop Some Financial Strategies For Yourself

Plan your expenses or, in a much better sense, strategize. When allowances or salaries come, you always have the urge to buy things you've fantasized about during times of financial "drought."

If you already have cash allocated for both these urges and the debts that need to be cleared , you won't get off course and get lost in your financial system. In other words, you won't get a migraine from piled up bills or worry if your next salary won't just end up as a payment for debts.

5. Avoid Splurging When You Are Low On Money

During the times of financial drought or difficulties, one can't help but fantasize on objects, activities, food, and other things that can't be had. It's one of the human race's natural flaws – to want something that's impossible to have. When someone is broke or is cutting down on expenses heavily, there's this feeling of being limited.

While it's true that some people are limited financially, it's not true that they are limited in happiness. However, money can buy almost anything that can make someone happy, instantly. This is the problem – instant. People seek instant pleasure and spending your money is always the solution.

So, whenever someone is short of money, that person feels deprived of this instant happiness that other people are getting. There is envy and there is an increasing desire to have something as soon as possible. It's like an addiction, so by the time the money arrives, people are so hungry to spend that they are able to do it daily without thinking about their budget.

What To Do: Control Your Urges

The simplest but most difficult and complicated solution is to control it. Not just when the money is finally available, but even when there is financial scarcity. It's natural to want things, but it's important to know if this desire is beneficial in the long run. True, that those boxes of cupcakes from the delicacy store last week are screaming for attention, and so are your taste buds, but are there no other options to satisfy your cravings without spending as much?

Sometimes people get blinded by the idea more than its purpose. Going back to the "cupcakes" example, a lot of items and foods on the market today are overpriced. Most of them have high prices because they are popular, branded, or are served in the comfort of a very fancy interior. The idea of sitting down in a restaurant that's adorned with shiny wooden walls and has a live band is sometimes more alluring than the idea of getting food to satiate hunger itself.

6. By Items That Are Fairly Priced

Try aiming for simple but fairly priced offerings. Let your cravings, desires, and decisions to save meet half way. Make a relationship out of them and learn to commit accordingly. In saving money, nobody is forced to save or banned from spending on pricey items. All you have to do is wisely choose what and where to spend money on. Most things are short-lived or forgotten easily, if you're going to spend a great deal of valuable money on something , that something should be just as valuable – both financially and personally.

__Conclusion__

Treat money as a sacred thing. It is something that comes and goes, but it never comes in the same way all the time. There are times of abundance and there are times of scarcity, you should be able to make the most of the plentiful times and save for the times when you will need it the most. It's true that money can be easy to come by, if you know how to earn it, but it's difficult to keep money.

Don't treat money as a means to get the things you want and need just for the moment. You should perceive money as a means of stability and security —built by saving and managing wisely, and not as an instant solution to satisfying one of your temporary urges.

The next step is to put this information to use, and begin saving more money today! Remember to approach your finances strategically, and plan what expenses are necessary. Save daily to reinforce your new relationship with money. And lastly, saving doesn't have to be boring. Reward yourself along the way with planned expenses that still fit in to your overall savings scheme.

Remember, aside from the usual techniques in saving money, like keeping it in your pocket, there are plenty other ways to cut down costs effectively. It's not just miscellaneous expenses or keeping yourself from getting broke that's getting in the way of effective saving. Some things at home, like electricity and food, contribute to your financial responsibilities. The key is learning how to prioritize your financial responsibilities.

Good luck with your financial future, I hope this book was able to give you some new ideas for saving money, and changed your attitude to money in some way!

About Us:

The Thought Flame is committed to add value to its customers through various books, online courses and other resources. You can learn more about us and our books at www.thethoughtflame.com.

Don't forget to check out our amazing **online video courses** at www.thethoughtflame.com/courses/ to take your knowledge to another level.

To check out our **extraordinary collection of diet/cookbooks**, visit http://www.thethoughtflame.com/category/non-fictional/cookbooks/ .

As a part of our valued relationship with our customers, we keep providing you free promotional books, courses and other stuff on subscribing with us on our site. We have a strict anti-spam policy and assure you no spam mails will be sent to your mailbox.

To subscribe with us, visit www.thethoughtflame.com.

Like our work and would like to say thanks?

Buy us a cup of coffee at www.thethoughtflame.com/coffee/

Author:

Amarpreet Singh is an avid learner and his passion for education has made him travel, work and study all across the world. He holds three masters degrees, including MBA, from top universities in Asia.

He is author of dozens of books, many of which are Amazon's bestseller, varying in various topics and categories. He also teaches many online courses having thousands of students across the world.

He has a keen interest in international affairs, economics, global poverty and politics, financial markets and entrepreneurship, and strives to be part of a community that shares the same passion.

He has worked as consultant with organizations like Airbus and The World Bank. He loves travelling and learning about new cultures, and has been fortunate to live/work/travel/study in countries like India, China, Korea, US, South Africa, Japan, Philippines, Singapore, Canada etc., and learn about the culture and lifestyle in each of them. To check out more of his work, visit www.thethoughtflame.com